THE BEST OF
Thai
COOKING

Best of Thai Cooking

Published in the U.K. by
EVANS MITCHELL BOOKS
17 Manchester Street,
London W1U 4DH.

Copyright © 2002 Evans Mitchell Books

ISBN: 1901268-03-9

Copy Editor: Gillian Sutch

Photographs on pages 4-5, 17, 23, 65, 71 and 74-75
Michael Freeman, London

Food Stylist: Supadee Ruangsakvichit

Photographs on pages 28 and 36 reproduced
courtesy of Centurion Books, London

Remaining photography:
Food prepared and photographed at
Cadmus Communications, Georgia, USA

Photographer: Marc Prpich

Art Director: Karen Mason

Food Stylists:
Angie Mosier
Chriscilla Wasson
Yasuko Iwatani

Assistant to the Stylists: Erin Bennett

Design: Centurion Press Ltd., London

Printed and Bound by
Rainbow Graphics and Printing Co., Hong Kong

THE BEST OF Thai COOKING

SUPADEE RUANGSAKVICHIT

Evans Mitchell Books

Contents

INTRODUCTION

Geographically, Thailand is at the crossroads of Asia so it is hardly surprising that other Eastern cultures have played a role in the development of the national cuisine. Unlike their neighbours, however, the Thais are blessed with a country free of a colonial past so what influences there have been have occurred slowly, naturally and as a matter of choice and have not detracted in any way from the distinctive and unique traditional flavours.

In the past two decades the growth in awareness and popularity of Thai food has been phenomenal and in high streets throughout the world more and more restaurants, ranging from small family-style eateries to large, opulent establishments, have been opening their doors to introduce this very special 'spicy-salty-sweet-sour' cuisine through such gastronomic delights as Tom Yam Kung (hot and sour prawn soup), Yam Pla Duk Full (deep-fried catfish with mango sauce), Kaeng Phed Gai (red curry chicken) and Tab Tim Krob (water chestnuts in coconut syrup).

A widely held, yet misconceived, idea about Thai food seems to be that it must be 'chilli hot'. Certainly, there are some dishes eaten with great gusto by the local people which may well cause unsuspecting 'first-timers' to momentarily gasp for air but generally the cooking technique is all about balance; a balance of spices, herbs, roots and leaves, carefully blended to enhance (rather than disguise, as is so often the case with Western sauces and additives) the natural flavours and textures of the main ingredients.

Indeed, if one were seeking a single-word summation of Thai food, the word would not be 'heat' but 'harmony'; a harmony of tastes, colours and textures, designed to appeal to the eye as well as the palate. Beside the qualities

of pleasing appearance and excellent taste, Thai food is also light and nutritious, as diametrically opposed to 'junk food' as it is possible to be and, as such, is very much a food of the present time; a time when the benefits of a more healthy diet are being universally acknowledged.

Within the following pages the author sets out to present a colourful guide to the preparation of some of the country's favourite dishes, introducing the cuisine to the uninitiated, whilst, hopefully, adding to the culinary repertoire of those already familiar with its appeal.

Chillies, both fresh and dried, are widely used in Thai cooking. Quantities should be adjusted according to personal taste. Those most frequently used in the following recipes are:
• Prik Khee Noo (small or bird's eye)
• Prik Chi Fa (medium to large)
• Prik Khee Noo Haeng (small dried)
• Prik Chi Fa Haeng (medium to large dried)
The Thai name (prik) is the same for red or green chillies.

In Thailand many of the spices, such as galangal, garlic and lemon grass are barbecued over hot coals prior to being pounded into a paste. This enhances the flavour of the individual spices, particularly so, when the ingredients are wrapped in a banana leaf (or tin foil). If this is not practical, place ingredients under a hot grill to char slightly.

To roast seeds, place in a heavy based pan and cook slowly for 10 minutes.

Mussaman Curry Paste

INGREDIENTS

3 dried chillies (prik chi fa haeng)
1 teaspoon coarsely chopped galangal, grilled
1 stalk lemon grass, grilled
4 cloves garlic, grilled
2 cloves, roasted
1 tablespoon coriander seeds, roasted
1 teaspoon cumin seeds, roasted
1/2 teaspoon peppercorns, roasted
6 shallots, sliced
1 teaspoon salt
1 teaspoon shrimp paste

Remove the seeds from the chillies and soak in water for 15 minutes, until soft, then slice finely. Chop the galangal, garlic and lemon grass.

Combine all the ingredients, except the shrimp paste, in a pestle and mortar, or blender, then add shrimp paste and process to a fine paste.

Choo Chee Curry Paste

INGREDIENTS

5 dried chillies (prik chi fa haeng)
1 tablespoon coarsely chopped galangal
1 stalk lemon grass, finely sliced
8 shallots, finely sliced
10 cloves garlic, finely sliced
1/2 teaspoon grated kaffir lime peel
1 teaspoon sliced coriander root
1 teaspoon shrimp paste

Remove the seeds from the chillies and soak in water for 15 minutes, until soft, then slice finely. Chop the galangal, garlic and lemon grass.

Slice the chillies and combine with all other ingredients except the shrimp paste, in a pestle and mortar or blender, then add the shrimp paste and process to a fine paste.

Panang Curry Paste

INGREDIENTS

- 5 dried chillies (prik chi fa haeng)
- 5 shallots, finely sliced
- 10 cloves garlic, finely sliced
- 1 tablespoon coarsely chopped galangal
- ½ stalk lemon grass, finely sliced
- ½ teaspoon grated kaffir lime peel
- ½ teaspoon white or black peppercorns
- 1 teaspoon sliced coriander root
- 1 teaspoon salt
- 1 teaspoon shrimp paste

Remove the seeds from the chillies and soak chillies in water for 15 minutes, until soft. Place all ingredients, except the shrimp paste, in a pestle and mortar or blender and combine. Add the shrimp paste and pound to a fine paste.

Kaeng Soom Curry Paste

INGREDIENTS

- 7 dried chillies (prik chi fa haeng)
- 5 shallots, finely sliced
- 5 cloves garlic, finely sliced
- 3 krachai stalks
- 2 teaspoons shrimp paste

Remove the seeds from the chillies and soak in warm water for 15 minutes, until soft.

Using a pestle and mortar, or blender, combine all the other ingredients, apart from the shrimp paste, then add the paste and process until smooth.

Roasted Chilli Paste

INGREDIENTS

- 4 tablespoons vegetable oil
- 6 cloves garlic, finely sliced
- 10 shallots, finely sliced
- 5 dried chillies (prik chi fa haeng)
- 2 tablespoons dried shrimps
- pinch of salt
- 1½ tablespoons palm sugar
- 1 tablespoon tamarind water

Heat a wok, add the vegetable oil and fry the garlic until golden, then remove and drain on kitchen paper. Repeat the process with the shallot and dried chillies. Place the dried shrimps in a pestle and mortar, or blender, and reduce to a powder. Add the garlic, shallots and chillies and process to a smooth paste. Re-heat the oil, add the paste and salt and stir-fry for 1 minute. Lower heat, add the palm sugar and tamarind water and continue to stir until the sauce thickens and becomes oily.

Green Curry Paste
Kaeng Kiew Warn

INGREDIENTS

- 15 fresh chillies (prik khee noo suan), finely sliced
- 1 tablespoon coriander seeds
- 1 teaspoon cumin seeds
- 10 shallots, finely sliced
- 5 cloves garlic, finely sliced
- 1 tablespoon coarsely chopped galangal
- 1 stalk lemon grass, finely sliced
- 1/2 tablespoon grated kaffir lime peel
- 1 teaspoon sliced coriander root
- 5 white or black peppercorns
- 1 teaspoon salt
- 2 teaspoons shrimp paste

Put the coriander seeds and cumin seeds in a cast iron frying pan and roast slowly, then allow to cool.

Using a pestle and mortar, or blender, combine all the ingredients, apart from the shrimp paste, then add the paste and process until smooth.

Red Curry Paste
Kaeng Phed Dang

INGREDIENTS

- 7 Dried chillies (prik khee noo haene), finely sliced
- 1 teaspoon cumin seeds
- 1 tablespoon coriander seeds
- 10 shallots, finely sliced
- 8 cloves garlic, finely sliced
- 1 tablespoon coarsely chopped galangal
- 1 stalk lemon grass
- 1/2 tablespoon grated kaffir lime peel
- 1 teaspoon sliced coriander root
- 1/2 teaspoon white or black peppercorns
- 1 teaspoon salt
- 1 teaspoon shrimp paste

Put the cumin and coriander seeds in a cast iron frying pan and roast slowly, then allow to cool.

Using a pestle and mortar, or blender, combine all the ingredients apart from the shrimp paste, then add the paste and process until smooth.

Prawn and Pork Coconut Dip with Rice Crackers

Khao Tung Na Tueng

INGREDIENTS

225 g fresh prawns
200 g fresh pork
3 coriander roots, chopped
3 cloves garlic, chopped
1 dried chilli (prik khee noo haeng),
    seeded, soaked and chopped
8 white peppercorns
2 teaspoons salt
300 ml thick coconut milk
1½ tablespoons palm sugar
2 tablespoons peanuts, roasted and ground
1 tablespoon chopped fresh coriander
350 g long-grain rice
oil for frying

Shell and de-vein the prawns, then mince. Mince the pork.

Place the coriander root, garlic, chilli, peppercorns and 1 teaspoon salt in a pestle and mortar, or blender, and combine to make a paste.

Place the coconut milk in a pan and heat until the oil separates, then add the spice paste and stir well to combine. Add the minced prawns and pork, together with the palm sugar, ground peanuts and remaining salt and cook for a further minute, stirring continuously.

Remove pan from the heat and allow mixture to cool, then transfer to a bowl and serve as a dip with rice crackers.

To make the crackers, cook the rice until tender and allow to cool.

Take tablespoons of the rice and shape into flat patties, approximately 2 cm in diameter. Place on a rack and bake in a very slow oven for 2 hours, turning occasionally, then remove and fry in hot oil until golden on both sides. Drain on kitchen paper and allow to cool.

Stuffed Taro

Pheak Yad Sai Tod

INGREDIENTS

200 g fresh prawns
450 g taro
150 g cornflour
oil for deep-frying
1 teaspoon salt
3 coriander roots, chopped
2 cloves garlic, chopped
8 whole white peppercorns
1 tablespoon diced onion
200 g crab meat, flaked
1 tablespoon rice wine
1 tablespoon light soy sauce
pinch of sugar

Shell, de-vein and mince the prawns.

Peel the taro and slice thinly. Steam until soft, then add 4 tablespoons cornflour, 1 tablespoon of oil and the salt and allow to cool. Knead for 5 minutes, then cover with a cloth and set aside.

Place the coriander root, garlic and peppercorns in a pestle and mortar, or blender, and combine to make a paste. Heat 1 tablespoon of oil in a wok and fry the paste until light brown, then add the onion, prawn and crab meat. Stir-fry for 2-3 minutes, then add the wine, soy sauce and sugar and continue to stir until the liquid has reduced and the mixture is fairly dry.

Flatten the taro and make into circles, approximately 5 cm in diameter. Place a teaspoon of the mixture in the middle of each circle and roll into an egg shape, then dust lightly with remaining cornflour.

Heat the oil in a wok until it starts to smoke, then reduce heat slightly, add the rolls and cook, in batches, until golden and crispy. Remove with a slotted spoon, drain on kitchen paper and transfer to a platter.

Shredded Dried Beef

Nuea Wan

INGREDIENTS

200 g boneless beef, finely sliced
2 1/2 tablespoons fish sauce
1/2 teaspoon ground black pepper
vegetable oil to fry
5 shallots, sliced
2 tablespoons sugar

Marinate the beef in the fish sauce and pepper for two hours. Lay on a rack and place in a slow oven (170°C/Gas mark 3), turning occasionally. Tenderise the meat by flattening it with a meat hammer, then cut into shreds.

Heat the oil in a pan and fry the shallot till crispy, then remove and drain on kitchen paper.

Re-heat the oil and fry the beef until it is crispy, then the sugar and half the shallot. Stir until the oil is syrupy and the beef is evenly coated, then transfer to a serving dish and garnish with the remaining shallot.

Thai Fish Cakes
Thod Mun Pla

INGREDIENTS

475 g white fish fillet
1½ tablespoons red curry paste
  (see page 9)
large pinch of salt
2 eggs, lightly whisked
1½ tablespoons fish sauce
60 g runner beans, finely sliced
3 kaffir lime leaves, shredded
oil for frying
50 fresh holy basil leaves

DIP

4 tablespoons sugar
3 tablespoons vinegar
1 teaspoon salt
2 shallots, thinly sliced
125 g cucumber, thinly sliced
1 tablespoon finely ground salted peanuts
1 chilli (prik chi fa), sliced and pounded

Remove any skin from the fish fillets and pass the flesh through a mincer into a mixing bowl. Add the curry paste and salt and mix well, then add the egg, fish sauce, chopped beans and lime leaves. Knead for 15-20 minutes, until the mixture is rubbery, then shape into patties, approximately 4 cm in diameter.

Heat the oil and fry the basil leaves until crispy. Remove with a slotted spoon, drain and set on one side. Re-heat the oil and fry the fish cakes, in batches, until cooked and golden on both sides. Remove with a slotted spoon, drain on kitchen paper and arrange on a serving platter. Garnish with the shredded basil leaves and serve with the dip.

To make the dip, put the sugar, vinegar and salt into a saucepan and bring to the boil, then lower the heat and simmer for approximately 10 minutes until it reduces and becomes syrupy. Allow to cool, then add the remaining ingredients and stir well.

Prawn Rolls
Kung Hom Pla

INGREDIENTS

12 large fresh prawns
2 coriander roots, chopped
4 cloves garlic, chopped
8 white peppercorns
1 teaspoon salt
1½ tablespoons soy sauce
1 tablespoon rice wine
12 rice wrappers
1 egg, lightly whisked
oil for deep-frying
75 g fresh pineapple chunks
sweet chilli sauce

Shell and de-vein the prawns, leaving the tails intact, then butterfly and place in a shallow dish.

Place coriander root, garlic, peppercorns and salt in a pestle and mortar, or blender, and combine into a paste, then add the soy sauce and wine and add to the prawns. Stir to ensure the prawns are evenly coated, then leave to marinate in the refrigerator for 1 hour.

Lay the wrappers on a flat surface. Drain the prawns and place one at the edge of each rice wrapper, leaving the tail protruding. Roll over once, fold excess wrapper over the prawn and continue rolling up tightly, then seal the edges with the egg.

Heat the oil in a wok and deep-fry the prawn rolls until golden, then remove with a slotted spoon and drain on kitchen paper. Arrange on a platter with the pineapple chunks and serve with a side dish of sweet chilli sauce.

Chicken in Pandan Leaves

Gai Haw Bai Toey

INGREDIENTS

500 g chicken breasts
3 cloves garlic, chopped
2 coriander roots, chopped
1 tablespoon white peppercorns
2 tablespoons light soy sauce
1 tablespoon rice wine
1 tablespoon sesame oil
1 1/2 tablespoons sugar
30 - 35 pandan leaves
oil for deep-frying
dipping sauce

Cut the chicken into bite-size pieces and place in a shallow bowl.

Pound the garlic, coriander and peppercorns to produce a paste, then combine with the soy sauce, wine, sesame oil and sugar. Add the mixture to the chicken and stir to coat evenly, then set aside in the refrigerator for 1 hour.

Lay the pandan leaves on a flat surface and place a piece of chicken in the centre of each. Fold into triangular shapes and tuck in the ends to secure.

Heat the oil in a wok until it starts to smoke and cook the chicken parcels in batches for 8-10 minutes. Remove with a slotted spoon and drain on kitchen paper, then transfer to a serving platter, unwrap and serve with a sweet and sour or chilli sauce for dipping.

Pork Satay

Moo Satay

INGREDIENTS

500 g pork fillet
1/2 teaspoon coriander seed
1/2 teaspoon cumin seed
1/2 teaspoon ground turmeric
5 white peppercorns
1 teaspoon salt
100 ml thick coconut milk
16 wooden satay sticks

SATAY SAUCE

3 dried chilli peppers (prik khee noo haeng), seeded, soaked and chopped
1 tablespoon chopped galangal
1 tablespoon chopped lemon grass
1/2 teaspoon salt
3 shallots, finely chopped
2 cloves garlic, finely chopped
400 ml thin coconut milk
4 tablespoons palm sugar
1 tablespoon fish sauce
4 tablespoons tamarind water
4 tablespoons salted peanuts, ground

CUCUMBER SALAD

3 tablespoons sugar
3 tablespoons vinegar
100 g cucumber, finely sliced
2 shallots, finely sliced
60 g carrot, finely sliced
1 fresh chilli (prik chi fa), finely sliced
1 teaspoon salt
1 tablespoon chopped fresh coriander

Slice the pork into thin pieces approximately 3 x 8 cm and place in a shallow dish. Place the coriander, cumin, turmeric, peppercorn and salt in a pestle and mortar, or blender, and combine into a paste. Rub the paste into the pork slices, then add 75 ml of coconut milk and leave to marinate for 1 hour.

Meanwhile, soak the satay sticks in cold water for 1 hour, then thread the pork onto the sticks (2-3 slices to each stick), ending 6 cm from the blunt end. Cook over hot charcoal, or under a grill, turning regularly and basting with remaining coconut milk, until tender and golden. Serve with satay sauce and cucumber salad.

To make the sauce, place the chilli, galangal, lemon grass and salt into a pestle and mortar, or blender, and combine into a rough paste. Add the shallot and garlic and continue to process until the paste is smooth.

Pour 75 ml of the coconut milk into a saucepan and heat until the oil separates out, then add the paste and mix well. Stir over a moderate heat for 2 minutes, then add the remaining coconut milk, palm sugar, fish sauce and tamarind water and continue to stir until the sauce thickens. Remove pan from the heat, stir in the ground peanuts and allow to cool slightly.

To make the cucumber salad, place the sugar and vinegar in a saucepan and bring to the boil. Lower heat and simmer for 10 minutes until the mixture become syrupy, then remove from the heat and allow to cool.

Finally add the cucumber, shallot, carrot, chilli, salt and coriander and combine well.

Seafood Soup with Lemon Grass

Tom Yam Poo Taek

INGREDIENTS

6 fresh king prawns
250 g baby squid
450 g white fish fillets
225 g scallops, shucked
225 g fresh crab meat
225 g fresh mussels, well scrubbed
800 ml chicken stock
4 tomatoes, quartered
200 g oyster or button mushrooms, sliced
3 kaffir lime leaves, shredded
1 tablespoon coarsely chopped galangal
3 lemon grass stalks, crushed and cut into
  3 cm long slices
4 fresh chillies (prik khee noo), finely sliced
1 teaspoon stir-fried chilli paste
  (see page 8)
2 tablespoons lime/lemon juice
fish sauce to taste
2 tablespoons chopped fresh coriander

Shell and de-vein the prawns, leaving the tails attached, then butterfly. Slice the squid, flake the fish, clean and cut the scallops in half and pick through the crab meat to ensure there are no remaining shell splinters.

Bring the chicken stock to a boil and cook the mussels until they open (discarding any that remain closed), then remove from the shells and set aside.

Add the tomato, mushroom, lime leaves, galangal and lemon grass to the stock and bring back to the boil, then add all the remaining seafood and lower the heat.

Allow to simmer for 3-4 minutes, then replace the mussels, add the chilli, chilli paste, lime juice and fish sauce and stir gently for a further 30 seconds.

Remove from the heat and transfer to a soup tureen, then sprinkle on the freshly chopped coriander.

Sweet and Sour Fish Soup

Pla Tom Soom

INGREDIENTS

150 g fresh mackerel fillets
5 shallots, chopped
2 teaspoons chopped coriander root
1 teaspoon minced garlic
½ teaspoon black peppercorns
1 tablespoon shrimp paste
large pinch of salt
1.2 litres fish stock
2 tablespoons finely sliced ginger
1 tablespoon tamarind water
1 tablespoon fish sauce
1 tablespoon palm sugar
5 spring onions, cut into 3 cm lengths
2 teaspoons chopped fresh coriander

Clean the fish and cut into serving size pieces.

Using a pestle and mortar, or blender, process the shallot, coriander root, garlic, peppercorns, shrimp paste and salt to produce a paste.

Heat the fish stock in a large saucepan, add the paste and stir well.

Bring to the boil, add the fish, taking care not to stir until the fish is cooked, then lower the heat, add the ginger, tamarind water, fish sauce and palm sugar and simmer for a few minutes.

Finally, adjust seasonings to taste, add the spring onion and cook for a further 30 seconds, then transfer to a tureen and garnish with chopped coriander.

Prawn and Vegetable Soup

Kaeng Liang

INGREDIENTS

12 fresh prawns
2 tablespoons dried shrimps
8 shallots, chopped
5 garlic cloves, chopped
2 fresh chillies (prik khee noo suan), chopped
1 tablespoon shrimp paste
1 tablespoon whole white peppercorns
large pinch of salt
900 ml chicken stock
175 g button mushrooms, sliced
150 g pumpkin, peeled and sliced
275 g baby spinach, shredded
150 g baby corn, sliced
125 g courgettes, sliced
1 tablespoon fish sauce
2 tablespoons hairy basil leaves

Shell and de-vein the prawns, leaving the tails attached.

Pound the dried shrimps to a powder. Add the shallot, garlic, chilli, shrimp paste, peppercorns and salt and combine to produce a paste.

In a large saucepan heat the chicken stock, add the paste and stir well, then bring to the boil. Add the prawns and cook for 2-3 minutes, then lower the heat, add the mushroom, pumpkin, spinach, corn and courgette and cook until tender.

Add the fish sauce and stir to blend, then add the basil leaves and cook for a further minute. Serve immediately.

Tip: This dish is hot because of the quantity of pepper and shallots, not the chillies, so adjust according to taste.

Spicy Prawn Soup

Tom Yam Kung

INGREDIENTS

8 fresh king prawns

600 ml chicken stock

2 tomatoes, quartered

200 g oyster mushrooms, sliced

3 kaffir lime leaves, shredded

1 tablespoon coarsely chopped galangal

2 lemon grass stalks, crushed and cut into
  3 cm long slices

1 teaspoon stir-fried chilli paste
  (see page 8)

4 fresh chillies (prik khee noo), finely sliced

2 tablespoons fresh lime juice

fish sauce to taste

fresh coriander leaves

Shell and de-vein the prawns, leaving the tails attached.

Bring the stock to a boil and add the tomato, mushroom, lime leaves, galangal and lemon grass. Bring back to the boil, then add the prawns, reduce the heat and cook until the prawns are tender.

Add the chilli paste, chilli, lime juice and fish sauce and stir well, then transfer to steamboat with the chimney filled with hot charcoal and garnish with fresh coriander.

Chicken Soup with Coconut and Galangal

Tom Kaa Gai

INGREDIENTS

2 chicken breasts fillets
500 ml thin coconut milk
2 stalks lemon grass, crushed and cut into
  3 cm long slices
1 tablespoon coarsely chopped galangal
3 kaffir lime leaves, shredded
250 ml chicken stock
200 g flat mushrooms, sliced
4 fresh chillies (prik khee noo), finely sliced
2 tablespoons fresh lime juice
1 tablespoon fish sauce
1 tablespoon chopped fresh coriander

Remove the skin from the chicken breasts and slice the meat.

In a saucepan, bring 50 ml of coconut milk to the boil and add the chicken. Cook for 3-4 minutes, turning occasionally, then slowly add the remaining coconut milk, add the lemon grass, galangal and lime leaves and bring back to the boil.

Stir for 2-3 minutes, then add the stock and bring back to the boil. Cook until the chicken is tender, then add the slices of mushroom and heat through.

Add the chilli, lime juice and fish sauce and stir well, then transfer to a tureen and sprinkle on the freshly chopped coriander.

Chicken Soup with Livers

Tom Yam Gai

INGREDIENTS

300 g chicken breast fillets
100 g chicken livers
salt and black pepper
1.2 litres chicken stock
2 shallots, finely sliced
25 mm knob ginger, finely sliced
2 teaspoons finely sliced lemon grass
2 teaspoons shredded kaffir lime leaves
2 teaspoons fresh lime juice

SEASONING SAUCE

3 fresh red chillies (prik knee noo),
  finely chopped
1 teaspoon finely chopped garlic
2 tablespoons sugar
2 tablespoons fish sauce
75 ml fresh lime juice

Slice the chicken breast and livers. Season with salt and pepper.

Bring the stock to the boil, add the shallot, ginger, lemon grass and lime leaves and cook for 1 minute, then add the chicken and the liver, lower heat and allow to simmer for 15-20 minutes.

Add the lime juice and stir for a further minute, then transfer to individual soup bowls and season to taste with the chilli-garlic sauce.

To make the sauce, blend the chilli, garlic and sugar until smooth, then add the fish sauce and lime juice and stir well.

Noodle Soup with Bean Curd and Minced Pork

Kaeng Jued Woon Sen Kub Tao Hoo

INGREDIENTS

- 100 g glass noodles
- 120 g dried Chinese mushrooms
- 175 g minced pork
- 1 teaspoon finely chopped garlic
- ½ teaspoon salt
- ½ teaspoon freshly ground black pepper
- 900 ml chicken stock
- 200 g fresh bean curd, diced
- 1 tablespoon light soy sauce
- 1 teaspoon freshly chopped coriander
- 2 spring onions, cut into 3 cm lengths

Soak the noodles in cold water for 20 minutes, then drain and cut into 3 cm lengths. Soak the mushrooms in warm water for 20 minutes, then discard the hard stems and quarter the caps.

Place the pork in a bowl, add the garlic, salt and pepper and mix well, then shape into small balls.

Bring the stock to the boil, add the pork balls and cook for 30 seconds. Lower the heat, add the noodles, mushrooms, bean curd and soy sauce and continue to cook for a further 15 minutes, frequently scooping off the fat which rises to the surface, ensuring the finished soup is as clear as possible.

Transfer the soup to a tureen, sprinkle with the coriander and garnish with spring onion.

Pumpkin and Coconut Soup
Kaeng Liang Fug Thong

INGREDIENTS

325 g fresh pumpkin
1 teaspoon fresh lime juice
75 g dried shrimps
2 shallots, chopped
2 fresh red chillies (prik khee noo),
  seeded and chopped
2 fresh green chillies (prik khee noo),
  seeded and chopped
1 teaspoon shrimp paste
250 ml thick coconut milk
750 ml thin coconut milk
salt to taste
2 teaspoons chopped hairy basil leaves

Peel the pumpkin roughly, leaving a little peel attached to prevent the flesh breaking up. Sprinkle with lime juice and set aside for 20 minutes.

Using a pestle and mortar, or blender, combine the dried shrimps, shallot and chilli, and process to produce a smooth paste. Bring the thick coconut milk to a boil in a saucepan, add the spice paste and cook for 5 minutes, stirring continuously, then lower heat and add the pumpkin.

Simmer for 10 minutes, then add half the thin coconut milk, season to taste with salt and bring back to the boil. Continue to cook until the pumpkin is tender (but not too soft), then add the remaining coconut milk and bring back to the boil.

Finally, add the basil leaves and stir for 30 seconds, then transfer to a tureen and serve immediately.

Stuffed Mushrooms in Clear Soup
Kaeng Jued Moo Sub Yad Sai Hed

INGREDIENTS

12 dried Chinese mushrooms
125 g finely minced lean pork
2 water chestnuts, finely chopped
1 teaspoon finely chopped coriander root
1 teaspoon finely chopped garlic
1 teaspoon finely chopped coriander leaves
2 teaspoons light soy sauce
2 teaspoons rice wine
salt and freshly ground black pepper
175 g water melon, seeded and roughly
  chopped
1.25 litres chicken stock
fresh coriander leaves

Soak the mushrooms in warm water for 20 minutes, then discard the hard stems.

Place the pork in a mixing bowl, add the water chestnut, coriander root, garlic, chopped coriander leaves, soy sauce, wine, salt and pepper and combine well.

Fill the mushroom caps with the mixture and cook in a steamer for 20 minutes, then transfer to a soup tureen. Add the pieces of water melon to the tureen.

Bring the stock to the boil, then transfer to the tureen and garnish with coriander leaves.

King Prawns with Noodles and Ginger
Kung Ob Mor Din

INGREDIENTS

8 king prawns
200 g glass noodles
3 coriander roots, chopped
2 cloves garlic, chopped
5 white peppercorns
½ teaspoon salt
1 tablespoon light soy sauce
2 teaspoons rice wine
1 tablespoon oyster sauce
1½ tablespoons finely chopped ginger
60 g pork fat, chopped
2 spring onions, finely chopped
150 g fresh shitake mushrooms
1 tablespoon chopped fresh coriander

Shell and de-vein the prawns, leaving the tail intact, then butterfly.

Soak the noodles in cold water until soft, then cut into 3 cm lengths and place in a bowl.

Using a pestle and mortar, or blender, process the coriander root, garlic, peppercorns and half the salt to produce a smooth paste.

Add the paste to the noodles, together with the soy sauce, wine, oyster sauce, remaining salt and ginger. Stir to combine and set aside for 15 minutes.

Arrange the pork fat in the bottom of a clay pot, add the noodle mixture, spring onions and shitake mushrooms, then lay the prawns on top and steam for approximately 20 minutes.

Transfer to a serving plate and sprinkle the chopped coriander on top.

Green Prawn Curry

Kaeng Kiew Warn Kung

450 g tiger prawns
4 tablespoons thick coconut milk
1 ½ tablespoons green curry paste
  (see page 9)
500 ml thin coconut milk
1 tablespoon fish sauce
½ teaspoon palm sugar
2 kaffir lime leaves
60 g pea aubergines
2 fresh chillies (prik chi fa), finely sliced
2 tablespoons sweet basil leaves

Shell and de-vein the prawns, leaving the tails attached.

Place the prawn heads in a pan, add 450 ml of water and bring to the boil. Simmer for 20 minutes, then strain the liquid and set aside.

Heat the thick coconut milk in a wok until the oil separates out, then remove 2 tablespoons and set aside. Add the curry paste to the wok and stir for 1 minute, then add the prawns and stir for a further minute.

Add the stock and thin coconut milk and bring to the boil, then add the fish sauce, palm sugar and lime leaves and continue to cook for 3 minutes over a high heat. Add the pea aubergine, lower the heat and simmer for 15 minutes, then add the chilli and basil leaves and remove pan from the heat.

Finally, fold in the reserved thick coconut milk, transfer to a warm dish and serve immediately.

Prawns with Chilli Paste

Kung Nueng Kub Prik Phao

INGREDIENTS

- 16 medium size prawns
- 2 shallots, chopped
- 2 teaspoons chopped ginger
- 2 teaspoons chopped red chilli
  (prik khee noo)
- 1 teaspoon chopped garlic
- 1 teaspoon chopped lemon grass
- 1 teaspoon chopped coriander root
- 1 teaspoon shrimp paste
- ½ teaspoon salt
- 6 black peppercorns
- 2 teaspoons fresh lime juice
- 175 ml thick coconut milk
- oil for frying

Shell and de-vein the prawns, leaving the tails attached, and place in a shallow dish.

Using a pestle and mortar, or blender, combine the shallot, ginger, chilli, garlic, lemon grass, coriander root, shrimp paste, salt and peppercorns and process until the paste is smooth.

Heat 2 tablespoons of oil, add the paste and stir. Add the lime juice and coconut milk and fry for a further 2 minutes until thoroughly mixed. Remove from heat.

Steam the prawns until cooked, then set aside.

Arrange the prawns on a platter and serve with a side dish of chilli sauce for dipping.

Prawn and Pineapple Curry

Kaeng Soon Kung Subparod

INGREDIENTS

500 g medium sized prawns

1½ tablespoons Kaeng Soom curry paste
  (see page 8)

900 g fresh pineapple, roughly sliced

1 tablespoon tamarind water

1½ tablespoons fish sauce

1 tablespoon lime/lemon juice

½ tablespoon palm sugar

Shell and de-vein the prawns, keeping the tails attached, then butterfly.

In a saucepan, bring 600 ml of water to the boil and cook the prawns until tender. Drain the prawns and reserve the water.

Place half the cooked prawns and the curry paste in a blender, or use a pestle and mortar, and process to a paste. Bring the reserved water back to the boil and add the prawn paste and pineapple, then lower heat and cook for 3-4 minutes.

Add the remaining prawns, tamarind water, fish sauce, lime juice and palm sugar and allow to simmer for a further 1-2 minutes, then transfer to a serving dish.

Choo Chee Curry with Prawns

Choo Chee Kung

INGREDIENTS

8 fresh king prawns

450 ml thick coconut milk

1½ teaspoons Choo Chee curry paste
  (see page 7)

1 tablespoon fish sauce

1 teaspoon palm sugar

1 fresh chilli (prik chi fa), finely sliced

2 kaffir lime leaves, shredded

1 tablespoon shredded sweet basil

Shell and de-vein the prawns, leaving the tails intact, then butterfly.

In a saucepan, heat 2 tablespoons of the coconut milk until the oil separates, then add the curry paste and stir well for 2-3 minutes. Add the prawns and cook for 2 minutes, then add the fish sauce, sugar and remaining coconut milk.

Stir until the sauce thickens, transfer to a serving dish and sprinkle the chilli, lime leaves and sweet basil on top.

Stuffed Crab Shells

Poo Ja

INGREDIENTS

2 cloves garlic, chopped
1 coriander root, chopped
1 tablespoon white peppercorns
450 g white crab meat
250 g minced pork
125 g shrimps, minced
3 tablespoons soy sauce
2 eggs, lightly whisked
8 crab shells, washed and dried
2 salted duck egg yolks, diced
1 tablespoon chopped fresh coriander
oil for deep-frying

Using a pestle and mortar, or blender, process the garlic, coriander root and peppercorns to produce a smooth paste.

Combine the crab meat, pork and shrimp in a bowl and gently fold in the paste. Add the soy sauce and half the egg and mix well.

Stuff the mixture into the crab shells, add a little of the diced egg yolk and a sprinkling of coriander. Cook in a steamer for 15 minutes, then allow to cool and top with the egg yolk. Brush the stuffed shells with the remaining whisked egg.

Heat the oil in a wok until it starts to smoke, then lower heat slightly and fry the stuffed shells until the surface is golden brown. Remove and drain off excess oil, then transfer to a large platter. Serve with a side dish of plum or chilli sauce.

Crab Coconut Curry

Poo Phud Prik Kaeng

INGREDIENTS

3 crabs
3 tablespoons vegetable oil
2 cloves garlic, minced
1 tablespoon red curry paste *(see page 9)*
200 ml thick coconut milk
2 teaspoons fish sauce
$^1/_2$ teaspoon salt
4 spring onions, finely sliced
2 fresh chillies (prik chi fa), sliced
freshly ground white pepper
1 tablespoon chopped fresh coriander

Clean the crabs and cut into quarters.

Heat the oil in a wok and fry the garlic until golden, then add the paste and stir well. Add the pieces of crab and stir-fry over a high heat for 2-3 minutes, then, continuing to stir, add the coconut milk, fish sauce and salt and cook for a further 10-12 minutes.

Finally, add the spring onion and chilli and stir well, then transfer to a serving dish, add a good grinding of pepper and garnish with freshly chopped coriander.

Mussels with Lemon Grass and Fresh Herbs
Hoy Ma Lang Pu Ob

INGREDIENTS

600 g mussels
3 stalks lemon grass, crushed and
  cut into 3 cm lengths
2 cloves garlic, minced
5 shallots, finely sliced
1/2 teaspoon salt
1 tablespoon rice wine/sherry
3 tablespoons sweet basil leaves

DIP

1 clove garlic, chopped
3 fresh chillies (prik chi fa), finely sliced
1/2 teaspoon salt
3 tablespoons fresh lime juice
1 1/2 teaspoons palm sugar
1 teaspoon chopped fresh coriander

Scrub the mussels and rinse in cold water. In a saucepan bring 200 ml of water to the boil, then add the mussels, lemon grass, garlic, shallot, salt and rice wine. Cover with a tightly-fitting lid and continue to cook until all the mussels are open, discarding any that remain closed.

Add the basil leaves and allow to simmer for 1 minute, then remove pan from the heat, drain the mussels and transfer to a warm dish.

To make the dip, combine the garlic, chilli and salt and pound until smooth, then add the lime juice, sugar and coriander and mix well.

Clams in Roasted Chilli Sauce
Hoy Lai Phad Maam Prik Phao

INGREDIENTS

500 g clams
3 tablespoons vegetable oil
1 clove garlic, minced
1 1/2 tablespoons roasted chilli paste
  (see page 8)
1/2 teaspoon salt
2 teaspoons soy sauce
1 tablespoon rice wine/sherry
2 fresh chillies (prik chi fa), finely sliced
2 tablespoons sweet basil leaves

Scrub the clams, rinse under cold water, then drain.

Heat the oil and fry the garlic until golden, then add chilli paste and stir well. Add the clams, salt, soy sauce and rice wine and stir continuously until the clams have opened, discarding any that remain closed.

Remove pan from the heat, add the chilli and basil leaves and stir for a further minute, then transfer to a warm dish and serve immediately.

Hot and Sour Seafood Pot

Tom Yam Ta Lay

INGREDIENTS

4 fresh medium size prawns
1 medium size crab
150 g sea bass fillets
150 g small squid
12 fresh mussels
1.2 litres chicken stock
2 pickled plums, halved
2 tablespoons fish sauce
2 tablespoons tamarind water
1 tablespoon light soy sauce
4 fresh red chillies (prik khee noo),
  finely sliced
2 tablespoons fresh lime juice
2 teaspoons palm sugar
freshly ground black pepper
fresh coriander leaves

Clean and prepare the seafood. Shell and de-vein the prawns, leaving the tails attached; chop the crab into 8 pieces; cut the sea bass and squid into bite-size pieces and scrub the mussels with a wire brush.

Pour the stock into a clay pot, or saucepan, and bring to the boil. Add the pickled plums, fish sauce, tamarind water and soy sauce and cook for 2-3 minutes.

Add the seafood and bring back to the boil. Cook for 2 minutes, then lower heat, add the chilli, lime juice, sugar and pepper and simmer until the seafood is cooked. Before serving, discard any mussels that have failed to open, then garnish with fresh coriander leaves.

Fish Ball Curry with Vegetables

Kaeng Pa Luk Chin Pla

INGREDIENTS

500 g white fish
1 tablespoon salt
2 tablespoons vegetable oil
1 tablespoon red curry paste
 (see page 9)
600 ml chicken stock
50 g round aubergine
50 g string beans, finely sliced
75 g baby corn, finely sliced
50 g krachai, peeled and finely sliced
3 kaffir lime leaves, shredded
1 teaspoon whole green peppercorns
2 tablespoons fish sauce
pinch of sugar
2 fresh chillies (prik chi fa), finely sliced
3 tablespoons holy basil leaves

Flake the fish and pound with the salt until smooth, then shape into 25-30 mm balls. Place in a bowl of iced water for 15 minutes.

Heat the oil in a saucepan and stir-fry the curry paste for 2 minutes, then add the fish balls and stir to coat evenly. Add the stock and bring to the boil, then add the vegetables, lime leaves and peppercorns.

Lower heat and simmer until the vegetables are tender, then stir in the fish sauce and sugar and continue to simmer until the sauce reduces.

Finally, add the chilli and basil leaves and cook for a further minute, then transfer to a platter and serve immediately.

Catfish Fritters with Mango Sauce

Yam Pla Duk Full

INGREDIENTS

350 g whole catfish
1 teaspoon salt
oil for deep-frying
5 dried chillies (prik khee noo)
lettuce leaves
1 tablespoon chopped fresh coriander
2 tablespoons salted peanuts

SAUCE

200 g green mangoes, grated
4 fresh chillies (prik khee noo suan),
 very finely sliced
6 shallots, finely sliced
2 tablespoon fresh lime juice
2 teaspoons fish sauce
1 teaspoon sugar

Wash the fish, rub with salt, rinse and pat dry. Cook in a steamer and allow to cool, then carefully remove all the bones and mash the flesh with a fork. Taking approximately 1 tablespoon of the fish, shape into small fritters.

Heat the oil in a wok and fry the chilli. Set on one side. Re-heat the oil and fry the fritters in batches until golden, then remove with a slotted spoon and drain on kitchen paper.

Place the lettuce leaves on a serving dish, arrange the fritters on top and garnish with the fried chillies, coriander and salted peanuts. Serve with a side dish of mango sauce.

To make the sauce, place the chilled mango in a bowl, add the chilli, shallot, lime juice, fish sauce and sugar and mix thoroughly.

Fish with Fresh Ginger Sauce
Pla Jiean

INGREDIENTS
- 500 g whole pomfret, or similar fish
- 1 teaspoon sea salt
- oil for deep-frying
- 12 shallots, finely sliced
- 8 cloves garlic, finely sliced
- 1 teaspoon fish sauce
- 2 teaspoons light soy sauce
- 2 teaspoons white bean sauce
- 2 tablespoons tamarind water
- 1 1/2 teaspoons palm sugar
- 125 g fresh ginger, finely sliced
- 2 fresh chillies (prik chi fa), finely sliced
- 2 spring onions, cut into 3 cm lengths
- fresh coriander leaves

Clean the fish and rub with salt, then rinse and pat dry. With a sharp knife make two incisions on each side of the fish, cutting well into the flesh.

Heat the oil and fry the whole fish until brown and crispy on both sides, then remove and drain on kitchen paper. Keep warm.

Heat 2 tablespoons fresh oil in the wok and stir-fry the garlic and shallot until crispy and golden, then remove, drain and set aside.

Re-heat the oil in the wok, add the fish sauce, soy sauce and bean sauce and stir well, then add the tamarind water and sugar and bring to the boil. Lower heat and allow to simmer until the sauce thickens, then add the ginger, chilli and spring onion and stir well.

Place the fish on a serving plate, sprinkle with the crispy garlic and shallot, pour on the sauce and garnish with fresh coriander.

Spicy Deep-Fried Garoupa
Pla Sam Rod

INGREDIENTS
- 500 g garoupa, or other firm white fish fillet
- 2 tablespoons sea salt
- oil for deep-frying
- 3 shallots, chopped
- 2 cloves garlic, chopped
- 2 fresh chillies (prik chi fa), finely sliced
- 60 ml tamarind water
- 1 1/2 tablespoons palm sugar
- 1 tablespoon fish sauce
- 2 tablespoons sweet basil leaves

Rub the fish with salt, then rinse and pat dry. With a sharp knife make two incisions on each side of the fish, cutting well into the flesh.

Heat the oil in a wok until it starts to smoke, then lower heat slightly and deep-fry the fish until it is fully cooked and the skin is golden and crispy, then remove and drain on kitchen paper. Place on a serving platter and keep warm.

Place the shallot, garlic and chilli in a pestle and mortar, or blender, and combine into a rough paste. Heat 2 tablespoons fresh oil in a wok add the paste and stir-fry for 1 minute, then, stirring continuously, add the tamarind water, sugar and fish sauce. Bring to the boil, then lower heat and simmer for 3 minutes, until the sauce thickens. Pour the sauce over the fish, garnish with fresh basil leaves and serve immediately.

Grilled Mackerel with Fresh Herbs
Pla Phao

INGREDIENTS

- 1 whole mackerel
- 1 teaspoon sea salt
- 1 tablespoon finely chopped shallot
- 1 teaspoon finely chopped galangal
- 1 teaspoon finely chopped lemon grass
- ½ teaspoon finely chopped kaffir lime leaves
- ½ teaspoon finely chopped sweet basil
- 1 tablespoon light soy sauce
- ½ teaspoon white pepper

DIP

- 2 teaspoons finely chopped red chilli (prik khee noo)
- ½ teaspoon finely chopped garlic
- ¼ teaspoon salt
- 2 teaspoons palm sugar
- 2 tablespoons fresh lime juice

Clean and gut the mackerel. Rub the skin with sea salt, then rinse and pat dry.

Combine the shallot, galangal, lemon grass, lime leaf, basil, soy sauce and pepper and stuff inside the cavity of the fish.

Wrap the fish in a banana leaf and cook under a hot grill for 15-20 minutes, then unwrap and serve with a chilli-garlic dip.

To make the dip, place the chilli, garlic and salt in a pestle and mortar, or blender, and process to a paste, then add the palm sugar and lime juice and stir until smooth.

Red Snapper with Chilli Sauce

Pla Nung Kub Prik Kaeng

INGREDIENTS

1 red snapper
2 tablespoons sea salt
3 tablespoons thick coconut milk
1 tablespoon red curry paste *(see page 9)*
½ teaspoon palm sugar
1 tablespoon fish sauce
1 kaffir lime leaf, shredded
1 fresh chilli (prik chi fa), finely sliced
1 tablespoon sweet basil leaves

Rub the snapper with the sea salt, then rinse and pat dry. Steam for 15 minutes and set aside.

Heat the thick coconut milk in a wok until the oil separates out, then remove 1 tablespoon and set aside. Add the red curry paste and stir for 2–3 minutes, then lower the heat and add the palm sugar, fish sauce and lime leaves. Stir well and simmer for a further 10 minutes.

Arrange the fish on a serving platter and serve with a side dish of chilli sauce.

Duck Stew
Ped Thun

INGREDIENTS

1.5 kg duck
1 teaspoon salt
1 teaspoon white pepper
1 1/2 tablespoons rice wine
2 teaspoons finely sliced ginger
2 cloves garlic
12 coriander roots
1 cinnamon stick, grilled
20 white peppercorns
2 tablespoons vegetable oil
600 ml chicken stock
4 spring onions, cut into 3 cm lengths
1 teaspoon soft brown sugar
2 tablespoons light soy sauce
1 tablespoon dark soy sauce
10 spring onions, cut into 3 cm lengths
1 teaspoon brown sugar
fresh coriander leaves

Cut the duck into chunks, including the bone. Place in a bowl, add the salt, pepper and rice wine and marinate for 30 minutes.

Wrap the ginger, garlic, coriander roots, cinnamon stick and peppercorns in a muslin cloth and tie securely.

Heat the oil in a wok and fry the duck until golden, then remove, drain and place in a large saucepan. Add the stock and the spice bag and bring to the boil. Lower heat and simmer until the duck is tender, frequently skimming off the fat which floats to the surface.

Increase the heat and continue to cook for a further 5 minutes to reduce the sauce, then add the spring onion, sugar and soy sauce.

Stir well, then transfer to a serving platter and garnish with fresh coriander leaves.

Duck Curry
Kaeng Phet Ped Yarng

INGREDIENTS

1 kg duck, roasted
400 ml coconut milk
1 tablespoon red curry paste *(see page 9)*
300 ml chicken stock
125 g cherry tomatoes
125 g pea aubergine
175 g lychees
1 tablespoon fish sauce
pinch of sugar
2 kaffir lime leaves, shredded
2 fresh chillies (prik chi fa), finely sliced
2 tablespoons sweet basil leaves

Cut the roast duck into pieces, including the bone.

Heat 100 ml of the thick coconut milk in a saucepan until the oil separates, then add the curry paste and stir well for 2-3 minutes. Add the duck and stir to coat evenly with the paste, then pour in the stock and remaining coconut milk and bring to the boil.

Lower the heat and continue to stir for a further 2 minutes, then add the tomato, aubergine, lychee, fish sauce, sugar and lime leaves and stir to combine.

Continue cooking over a low heat until the duck is tender, then add the chilli and basil leaves, remove from the heat and transfer to a serving dish.

Chicken with Fresh Ginger
Gai Phad Khieng

INGREDIENTS

300 g chicken breasts
2 teaspoons sesame oil
2 teaspoons light soy sauce
pinch of sugar
1 tablespoon rice wine
oil for frying
2 cloves garlic, minced
1 large onion, finely sliced
125 g wood ear mushrooms,
    soaked then sliced
150 g ginger, finely sliced
2 spring onions, cut into 3 cm lengths
1 fresh chilli (prik chi fa), finely sliced
freshly ground white pepper
1 tablespoon chopped fresh coriander

Finely slice the chicken and place in a bowl. Add the sesame oil, soy sauce, sugar and rice wine and marinate for 15 minutes.

Heat a wok, add some oil and fry garlic until light brown. Drain the chicken and add to the wok along with the onion. Stir-fry for a few minutes, then add the mushroom and ginger and continue to stir until the chicken is cooked.

Add the spring onion and chilli, stir well together and remove from the heat, then transfer to a serving plate, add a good grating of pepper and garnish with fresh coriander.

Chicken Casserole
Tom Kem Gai

INGREDIENTS

8 chicken thighs
freshly ground black pepper
2 tablespoons rice flour
4 dried chinese mushrooms
2 shallots, chopped
1 teaspoon garlic
1 teaspoon chopped galangal
1/2 teaspoon chopped coriander root
1/4 teaspoon salt
50 ml vegetable oil
50 g soft brown sugar
1 tablespoon light soy sauce
4 hard boiled eggs, halved

Season the chicken with pepper, then coat with flour. Soak the mushrooms in warm water for 20 minutes, then discard the hard stems.

Using a mortar and pestle, or blender, combine the shallot, garlic, galangal, coriander root and salt and process to a smooth paste.

Heat the oil in a casserole dish, add the paste for 5 minutes, to give flavour to the oil, then discard the paste. Add the sugar to the dish and stir until the oil becomes syrupy, then add the soy sauce and 250 ml of cold water.

Bring to the boil, add the chicken and mushrooms and cover the dish.

Lower the heat and simmer for 1 hour, then add the eggs and continue to cook for a further 15-20 minutes, until the chicken is fully cooked.

Red Curry Chicken

Kaeng Phed Gai

INGREDIENTS

- 500 g chicken breast fillets
- 600 ml thick coconut milk
- 1 ½ tablespoons red curry paste
  (see page 9)
- 275 ml chicken stock
- 375 g bamboo shoots, sliced
- 6 round aubergine, sliced
- 2 kaffir lime leaves, shredded
- 1 teaspoon sugar
- 2 fresh chillies (prik chi fa), finely sliced
- 2 tablespoons sweet basil leaves

Slice the chicken breasts.

Heat the coconut milk in a pan until the oil separates, then remove 2 tablespoons and set aside. Add the curry paste to the pan and stir well. Add the chicken and stir to ensure the slices are evenly coated with the paste, then pour in the stock and remaining coconut milk and bring to the boil.

Cook over a high heat for 3 minutes, then lower heat, add the bamboo shoots and simmer for 20 minutes. Then, add the aubergine, lime leaves, and sugar and cook for 10 more minutes.

Finally add the chilli, basil and reserved coconut milk and stir well, then remove from the heat, transfer to a bowl and serve immediately.

Spicy Chicken with Quail Eggs
Gai Thod Kruen Ted

INGREDIENTS

500 g chicken breast fillets
5 dried Chinese mushrooms
2 cloves garlic, chopped
3 coriander roots, chopped
1 teaspoon white peppercorns
500 ml chicken stock
1 tablespoon five-spice powder
2 teaspoons light soy sauce
2 teaspoons dark soy sauce
1 tablespoon palm sugar
12 hard boiled quail eggs, halved
75 ml vegetable oil
200 g bean curd, cubed

Cut the breasts in half. Soak the mushrooms in warm water for 20 minutes, then discard the stems and cut the caps into quarters. Using a pestle and mortar, or blender, combine the garlic, coriander and peppercorns and process to a smooth paste.

Heat the stock in a saucepan, stir in the paste and the five-spice powder and bring to the boil. Add the chicken and cook for 15 minutes over a high heat, then reduce the heat and add the mushrooms and the soy sauce. Cook for 15 minutes, then add the palm sugar and the eggs and simmer for a further 20 minutes. Remove the chicken and eggs and set aside to cool.

Heat half the oil in a frying pan and fry the bean curd until golden, then remove and drain on kitchen paper. Add the remaining oil to the pan, re-heat and fry the chicken, turning occasionally, until golden, then remove and drain. Arrange the chicken on a serving platter, surround with bean curd and garnish with the quail eggs.

Stuffed Chicken Breasts
Og Gai Sod Sai

INGREDIENTS

2 chicken breast fillets
2 teaspoons dark soy sauce
2 cloves garlic, chopped
2 coriander roots, chopped
1 teaspoon black peppercorns
300 g minced pork
6 button mushrooms, finely sliced
1 small onion, finely chopped
1 water chestnut, finely sliced
1 teaspoon garlic paste
1 tablespoon rice flour
1 egg, lightly whisked
2 teaspoons light soy sauce
oil for frying
fresh coriander leaves

Slice the chicken breasts in half and pound to flatten slightly. Place in a shallow dish, add the dark soy sauce and let stand for 15 minutes.

Using a mortar and pestle, or blender, process the garlic, coriander root and pepper into a smooth paste.

Combine the pork, mushroom, onion, water chestnut, flour, garlic paste, egg and light soy sauce. Mix well and spread evenly over the chicken slices, then roll up and secure with kitchen thread. Chill in the refrigerator for 1 hour.

Heat the oil in a wok until it is very hot, then add the chicken and cook until tender, turning frequently to ensure an even golden appearance. Remove and drain on kitchen paper. Remove kitchen thread then transfer to a serving plate and garnish with crispy, fried coriander leaves and sweet dipping sauce.

Beef Mussaman

Kaeng Mussaman Nuea

INGREDIENTS

500 g beef steak
450 ml thick coconut milk
1 tablespoon Mussaman curry paste,
  (see page 7)
125 g onions, coarsely chopped
125 g potatoes, peeled and cut into chunks
2 tablespoons fried peanuts
3 cardamom leaves
3 cardamom seeds, grilled
1 cinnamon stick, grilled
1 1/2 tablespoons fish sauce
2 - 3 tablespoons tamarind water
1/2 tablespoon palm sugar

Cut the beef into bite-size chunks.

Heat 200 ml of the coconut milk in a saucepan until the oil separates, then add the curry paste and stir for 3-4 minutes. Add the beef and stir to coat evenly, then pour in the remaining coconut milk and bring to the boil.

Reduce the heat, add the onion, potato, peanuts, cardamom leaves, cardamom seeds and cinnamon, and continue to simmer until the beef is tender and the sauce has reduced and thickened, taking care not to overcook the potato and onion.

Add the fish sauce, tamarind water and sugar and adjust seasonings to taste, then transfer to a dish and serve immediately.

Curried Meats Northern Style

Kaeng Hung Lay

INGREDIENTS

225 g lean pork
225 g lean chicken
2 tablespoons oil
2 teaspoons minced garlic
1 tablespoon red curry paste, *(see page 9)*
150 ml thick coconut milk
500 ml chicken stock
1/2 teaspoon salt
3 dried red chillies, (prik khee noo hang),
  soaked, seeded and chopped
50 g fresh ginger, finely sliced
1/2 teaspoon ground turmeric
2 teaspoons fresh lime juice
2 tablespoons fish sauce
1 teaspoon palm sugar
julienne strips of fresh red chillies
  (prik chi fa)
4 pickled garlic cloves, finely chopped

Cut the pork and chicken into bite-size chunks.

Heat the oil in a wok and fry the garlic until golden, then add the curry paste and stir well. Add the coconut milk, stir until the liquid is reduced and thickened, then add the meat, stock, salt and simmer until almost cooked.

Add the chillies, ginger, turmeric, lime juice, fish sauce, palm sugar and pickled garlic and bring back to the boil. Continue to cook until the meat is tender, then transfer to a serving dish and garnish with strips of fresh red chilli.

Pork Balls with Asparagus

Phad Loog Chin

INGREDIENTS

4 dried Chinese mushrooms
500 g minced pork
2 shallots, chopped
1 teaspoon chopped garlic
1 teaspoon chopped coriander root
1 teaspoon sugar
salt and white pepper
1 tablespoon light soy sauce
1 egg, lightly whisked
2 water chestnuts, finely chopped
75 g bamboo shoot, finely chopped
50 g plain flour
150 g asparagus spears
200 g mushrooms, sliced
100 g ginger, sliced
oil for deep frying
fresh coriander leaves

Soak the mushrooms in warm water for 20 minutes, then discard the hard stems and finely chop the caps.

Heat a little oil in a frying pan and stir fry the pork for 3-4 minutes, then place in a bowl and leave to cool.

Using a mortar and pestle, or blender, combine the shallot, garlic, coriander root, sugar, salt, pepper and soy sauce and process to produce a smooth paste.

Add the paste to the pork, together with the egg, mushroom, water chestnut and bamboo shoot. Stir to blend thoroughly and shape into small balls, approximately 25 mm in diameter, then coat with flour and place in the refrigerator for 30 minutes.

Stir-fry the asparagus, mushrooms and ginger.

Heat the oil until it starts to smoke, then lower heat slightly and fry the pork balls until golden. Remove with a slotted spoon and drain on kitchen paper, then transfer to a serving plate, surround with the stir-fried asparagus and garnish with fresh coriander leaves.

PHOTOGRAPH OVERLEAF

Beef with Chilli and Holy Basil
Phad Bai Krai-Phao Nuea

INGREDIENTS

275 g rump steak
2 tablespoons oil
2 cloves garlic, crushed and finely chopped
6 fresh chillies (prik chi fa), finely sliced
75 g dwarf, or runner beans, sliced
1 tablespoon fish sauce
2 tablespoons oyster sauce
1 tablespoon dark soy sauce
1 teaspoon sugar
1 teaspoon ground white pepper
2 tablespoons holy basil leaves

Cut the beef into thin slices.

Heat the oil in a wok and stir-fry the garlic and chilli for 3 minutes, then add the beef and stir continuously for 30 seconds.

Add the beans, fish sauce, oyster sauce, soy sauce and sugar and keep stirring for 3 minutes. Add the basil leaves and adjust seasonings to taste, then transfer to a warm dish and serve immediately.

Dry Aromatic Beef Curry
Panang Nuea

INGREDIENTS

175 ml thick coconut milk
1½ tablespoons Panang curry paste
 (see page 8)
500 g topside beef, thinly sliced
125 ml beef stock
100 g pea aubergines
2 tablespoons fish sauce
1 teaspoon palm sugar
2 fresh chillies (prik chi fa), thinly sliced
8 sweet basil leaves

Heat the thick coconut milk in a saucepan until the oil separates, then remove 1 tablespoon and set aside. Add the curry paste to the pan and stir well for 2-3 minutes, then add the beef and stir to coat evenly with the sauce.

Add the stock and the remaining coconut milk and bring to the boil. Cook for 3 minutes over a high heat, then lower heat and add the aubergines, fish sauce and sugar.

Simmer for 20 minutes until the sauce is reduced and thickened, then remove the pan from the heat. Add the chilli and basil leaves and stir well, then transfer to a serving dish and top with the reserved coconut milk.

Green Curry Vegetables

Kaeng Khew Warn Ja

INGREDIENTS

400 ml thick coconut milk
1 tablespoon green curry paste *(see page 9)*
75 g pumpkin, finely sliced
50 g round aubergine, finely sliced
75 g bamboo shoots, finely sliced
50 g courgette, finely sliced
50 g mangetout, finely sliced
50 g okra, sliced in half
1 fresh chilli (prik chi fa), finely sliced
2 tablespoons sweet basil leaves

Heat the coconut milk in a saucepan until the oil separates, then remove 2 tablespoons and set aside. Add the green curry paste to the pan and stir well for 2 minutes, then lower heat, add the vegetables and cook until tender.

Stir in the reserved coconut milk, add the chilli and basil and cook for a further minute, then transfer to a dish and serve immediately.

Spinach with White Bean Sauce

Phad Puk

INGREDIENTS

300 g spinach, chopped
1 tablespoon white bean sauce
2 tablespoons vegetable oil
2 teaspoons finely chopped garlic
2 fresh chillies (prik khee noo), finely sliced
2 tablespoons oyster sauce
1 teaspoon fish sauce
freshly ground black pepper

Place the spinach in a bowl and top with the bean sauce. Set aside for 10 minutes.

Heat the oil in a wok and stir-fry the garlic and chilli for 2-3 minutes, then add the spinach and oyster sauce and cover the pan for 15 seconds.

Uncover and stir over a high heat for 2 minutes, then stir in the fish sauce. Cook for a further 15 seconds, then transfer to a serving dish and top with a good grinding of black pepper.

Broccoli in Oyster Sauce

Phad Pak Naam Mun Hoy

INGREDIENTS

400 g broccoli
2 tablespoons vegetable oil
1 teaspoon finely chopped garlic
60 ml oyster sauce
1 tablespoon light soy sauce
freshly ground white pepper

Break the broccoli into florets and discard the hard stems. Cook in a steamer for 3-4 minutes.

Heat the oil in a wok and fry the garlic until golden and crispy, then add the broccoli. Cook for 2 minutes, stirring frequently, then add the oyster sauce, soy sauce and pepper. Stir and cook for a further 30 seconds, then transfer to a vegetable dish and serve immediately.

Bean Sprouts with Bean Curd

Thua Ngok Paad Tao Hoo

INGREDIENTS

150 g bean sprouts
200 g fresh bean curd
3 spring onions
2 tablespoons oil
2 teaspoons crushed garlic
1 tablespoon oyster sauce
1 tablespoon light soy sauce
2 teaspoons finely sliced fresh chilli
  (prik chi fa)
freshly ground black pepper

Trim the bean sprouts, dice the bean curd and cut the spring onions into 3 cm lengths.

Heat half the oil in a wok and fry the garlic until golden, then add the bean curd and stir for 2 minutes.

Add the remaining oil and re-heat, then add the bean sprouts, oyster sauce and soy sauce and continue stirring for a further minute.

Finally, add the spring onion and chilli and stir to mix, then transfer to a serving plate and add a grinding of black pepper. Dice the bean curd.

Heat the oil and fry the garlic until brown, add the bean curd and stir until golden. Add the remaining ingredients except for the spring onions and chilli. At the end, add the chilli and garlic, cook for 1 minute and remove from heat.

PHOTOGRAPH OVERLEAF

Prawn Salad with Lemon Grass
Plar Kung

INGREDIENTS

- 12 medium - large prawns
- 3 - 4 cloves garlic, minced
- 5 fresh chillies (prik khee noo suan), finely sliced
- 1 teaspoon salt
- 3 tablespoons fresh lime juice
- 2 teaspoons fish sauce
- 1 teaspoon grilled chilli paste *(see page 8)*
- pinch of sugar
- 4 stems lemon grass, finely sliced
- 10 shallots, finely sliced
- 4 spring onions, finely sliced
- 10 mint leaves
- 1 tablespoon freshly chopped coriander
- 4 kaffir lime leaves, finely sliced

Shell and de-vein the prawns, leaving the tails intact, then butterfly.

Boil until almost cooked, then drain and place in a bowl.

Using a pestle and mortar, or a blender, process the garlic and chillies into a rough paste. Add lime juice, fish sauce, chilli paste and sugar and mix well. Adjust seasonings to taste and pour over the prawns.

Mix lightly, then add the lemon grass, shallot and spring onion and toss well. Arrange on a serving plate and garnish with mint leaves, coriander and shredded lime leaves.

Spicy Smoked Mackerel Salad
Mieng Pla Too

INGREDIENTS

- 225 g smoked mackerel
- 1 tablespoon lime/lemon juice
- 1 teaspoon fish sauce
- 1 teaspoon salt
- 4 fresh chillies (prik khee noo suan), finely sliced
- 10 shallots, finely sliced
- 125 g fresh ginger, finely sliced
- 4 spring onions, finely sliced
- 150 g salted peanuts, lightly crushed
- 20 mint leaves

Grill the smoked mackerel until hot, de-bone and remove the skin. Flake the flesh into a bowl. Add the lime juice, fish sauce, salt and chillies and stir well.

Add the shallot, ginger and spring onion and toss lightly, then sprinkle with salted peanuts and garnish with mint leaves.

Seafood Salad

Yam Talay

INGREDIENTS

150 g white fish fillet, boiled
150 g boiled squid
125 g cooked prawns
1 small red onion, finely sliced
3 spring onions, cut into 3 cm lengths
2 stalks Chinese celery, finely sliced
10 cherry tomatoes, quartered
75 g wood-ear mushrooms, soaked and sliced
3 cloves garlic, chopped
3 fresh chillies (prik khee noo suan), sliced
pinch of salt
2 tablespoons lime juice
1 tablespoon fish sauce
1 teaspoon sugar
lettuce leaves
1 tablespoon chopped fresh coriander
10 mint leaves

Cut the fish into bite-size chunks and place in a salad bowl. Cut the squid into rings and add to the bowl. Shell and de-vein the prawns and place in the bowl, then add the red onion, spring onion, celery, tomato and mushroom

Using a mortar and pestle, or blender, combine the garlic, chillies and salt and process to produce a smooth paste, then add the lime juice, fish sauce and sugar and stir to blend.

Add the paste to the salad and toss lightly. Arrange the lettuce leaves on a plate, top with the salad and a sprinkling of freshly chopped coriander and mint leaves.

Beef and Aubergine Salad

Yam Nuea Ma Khea Orn

INGREDIENTS

500 g rump steak
1 tablespoon dark soy sauce
2 cloves garlic, chopped
3 fresh chillies (prik chi fa), sliced
2 tablespoons lime juice
2 teaspoons fish sauce
$\frac{1}{2}$ teaspoon sugar
8 small round aubergines, thinly sliced
1 onion, thinly sliced
8 cherry tomatoes, halved
3 spring onions, cut into 3 cm lengths
fresh coriander leaves

Place the beef in a shallow dish, pour on the dark soy sauce and leave for 30 minutes.

Pound the garlic and chilli into a paste, then add the lime juice, fish sauce and sugar and combine well.

Heat a non-stick frying pan and seal the beef on both sides for a few seconds, then transfer to a hot grill and cook for 3-4 minutes, turning once (the meat should be pink). Allow the meat to cool, then cut into very thin slices.

Place the aubergine, onion, tomato and spring onion in a salad bowl.

Add the beef and pour on the sauce, then toss lightly and garnish with fresh coriander.

Hot and Sour Pomelo Salad
Yam Som O

INGREDIENTS

6 medium size prawns
75 g fresh coconut, finely sliced
2 tablespoons vegetable oil
2 cloves garlic, finely sliced
2 shallots, finely sliced
2 tablespoons thick coconut milk
1 tablespoon roasted chilli paste
  (see page 8)
2 tablespoons lime juice
1 tablespoon fish sauce
1 teaspoon sugar
2 fresh chillies (prik chi fa),
  finely sliced
1 pomelo, segmented
1 tablespoon ground salted peanuts
125 g boiled chicken breast, shredded
fresh coriander leaves

Shell and de-vein the prawns, leaving their tails intact, then butterfly and cook in boiling water for 30 seconds.

Heat a wok, and dry-fry the coconut slices for 5-10 minutes until light brown.

Heat the wok and fry the garlic slices until crispy. Remove and drain on kitchen paper and repeat the process with the shallot slices.

Heat the coconut milk in a pan, add the roast chilli paste and stir well, then lower heat and continue to stir until the sauce thickens. Remove from the heat, add the lime juice, fish sauce, sugar and chilli and mix well, then transfer to a bowl and allow to cool.

Add the pomelo segments and mix together, then transfer to a salad bowl, sprinkle with ground peanut, top with shredded chicken and prawns and garnish with coriander leaves.

Papaya Salad with Sticky Rice
(Northeast Style)
Khao Neaw Som Tum

INGREDIENTS

200 g glutinous rice
900 g green papaya
125 g dried shrimps
6 cloves garlic, chopped
6 fresh chillies (prik khee noo)
175 g cherry tomatoes, halved
3 tablespoons tamarind water
3 tablespoons fish sauce
2 tablespoons fresh lime juice
3 tablespoons palm sugar

Soak the rice overnight, then drain in a muslin cloth and steam until fully cooked.

Shred the papaya. Pound the dried shrimps to a fine powder.

Using a pestle and mortar, or blender, combine the garlic and chilli and process to a rough paste. Add the powdered shrimp and one quarter of the tomato and grind together, then add the tamarind water, fish sauce, lime juice and sugar and stir to combine well.

Add the papaya and remaining tomato and combine well. Transfer the salad and rice to a dish and serve immediately.

Salad with Dried Seafood and Cashews

Yam Sarm Krob

INGREDIENTS

- oil for deep-frying
- 10 shallots, finely sliced
- 125 g dried squid
- 125 g dried shrimps
- 125 g cashew nuts
- 2 sticks Chinese celery, finely sliced
- 1 teaspoon crushed garlic
- 3 fresh chillies (prik khee noo suan), sliced
- pinch of salt
- 1 tablespoon lime/lemon juice
- 2 teaspoons fish sauce
- pinch of sugar
- lettuce leaves
- fresh coriander leaves

Heat the oil in a saucepan and fry the shallots until golden brown and crispy, then remove and drain on kitchen paper. Do likewise with the squid, shrimps and cashews, frying each separately. Allow all to cool, then place in a bowl and add the celery.

Using a mortar and pestle, or blender, process the garlic, chilli and salt into a rough paste. Add the lime juice, fish sauce and sugar and stir to blend, then add to the salad and toss lightly.

Transfer to a platter lined with the lettuce leaves and garnish with fresh coriander.

Thai Chef Salad

Yam Yai

INGREDIENTS

- 125 g prawns
- 125 g squid
- 75 g pork fillet, shredded
- 125 g chicken breast, shredded
- 3 cloves garlic
- 3 chillies (prik khee noo)
- pinch of salt
- 2 tablespoons lime juice
- 1½ tablespoons fish sauce
- pinch of sugar
- 3 spring onions, cut into 3 cm lengths
- 1 onion, finely sliced
- 2 chinese celery stalks, sliced
- 10 cherry tomatoes, cut in half
- 75 g wood-ear mushrooms,
- lettuce leaves soaked and sliced
- 1 tablespoon chopped coriander

Shell and de-vein the prawns, leaving the tails attached. Butterfly the prawns, boil for a few seconds, then drain and leave to cool. Clean the squid, cut into rings and boil. Boil the pork for a few seconds, then drain, leave to cool and cut into fine shreds.

Using a mortar and pestle or blender, process the garlic, chillies and salt into a paste. Add the lime juice, fish sauce, sugar and mix well. Add the paste to the meats in a bowl, stir together then add the remaining ingredients and toss together.

Place the lettuce on a serving plate, top with the salad mix and garnish with coriander leaves.

Winged Bean Salad
Yam Thau Plu

INGREDIENTS

12 fresh prawns
300 g pork fillet, shredded
300 g winged or string beans, finely chopped
75 g fresh coconut, finely sliced
oil for frying
2 shallots, finely sliced
2 cloves garlic, finely sliced
2 tablespoons thick coconut milk
1 tablespoon stir-fried chilli paste
  (see page 8)
2 fresh chillies (prik khee noo), finely sliced
2 tablespoons lime juice
1 tablespoon fish sauce
1 teaspoon palm sugar
4 dried chilies (prik khee noo haeng), fry

Shell and de-vein the prawns, leaving the tails attached. Butterfly the prawns and boil until tender, then drain and leave to cool.

Pour a little water into a pan, add a pinch of salt and cook the beans for 2–3 minutes. Remove and plunge into iced water for a few seconds, then drain, allow to cool and place in salad bowl.

Heat a wok and dry fry the coconut slices until golden, then remove and set aside. Add the oil to the wok and bring to a high heat. Fry the shallot and garlic until crispy, then remove and drain on kitchen paper.

Heat the coconut milk in a saucepan and add the chilli paste. Stir well, then lower heat and simmer until the sauce thickens. Remove pan from the heat, then stir in the lime juice, fish sauce and sugar. Allow to cool.

Pour the sauce over the beans and toss well, then top with the coconut, shallot, garlic and chilli and arrange the prawns around the sides of the bowl and fried chillies.

Herbed Fruit Salad
Yam Phol La Mai

INGREDIENTS

8 large fresh prawns
3 fresh chillies (prik chi fa), sliced
2 cloves garlic, chopped
1/2 teaspoon salt
2 tablespoons fresh lime juice
1 teaspoon fish sauce
oil for frying
8 shallots, finely sliced
1 green apple, diced
50 g grapes, seeded and halved
75 g diced pineapple
1 green mango, diced
6 cherry tomatoes, finely sliced
pinch of sugar
8 mint leaves
8 fresh coriander leaves

Shell and de-vein the prawns and cut in half lengthways. Boil for a few seconds, then drain and allow to cool.

Using a mortar and pestle, or a blender, process the chilli, garlic and salt into a smooth paste. Add the lime juice and fish sauce and stir to combine.

Heat the oil in a wok and fry the shallot until crispy and golden, then remove with a slotted spoon and drain on kitchen paper.

In a large bowl combine all the fruit and cherry tomatoes. Add the chilli sauce and toss together. Add the prawns and sugar and toss again. Garnish with mint and coriander.

PHOTOGRAPH OVERLEAF

Taro with Coconut Milk
Pua Kaeng Buad

INGREDIENTS

350 g taro
3 teaspoons salt
400 ml thick coconut milk
2 tablespoons palm sugar

Peel the taro and cut into bite-size slices and place in a bowl. Add most of the salt and cover with cold water. Leave for 30 minutes, then drain. Set aside 2 tablespoons of coconut milk and pour the remainder into a saucepan. Add the taro and bring to the boil, then lower heat, and stir in the sugar and remaining salt. Allow to simmer, stirring frequently, then stir in the reserved coconut milk and transfer to a serving bowl.

Pumpkin Custard
Sankaya Fuctong

INGREDIENTS

1 medium size pumpkin
400 ml coconut milk
2 tablespoons palm sugar
pinch of salt
3 eggs
2 pandan leaves, cut into 8 cm lengths

Carefully cut off the top of the pumpkin and scoop out the seeds.

Pour the coconut milk into a bowl, add the palm sugar, salt, eggs and pandan leaves and mix well. Squeeze the pandan leaves to extract the flavour, then discard.

Whisk the mixture until it is smooth, then pour into the pumpkin and steam for 20-25 minutes, until the custard is set.

Coconut Ice-Cream

Ai Tim Gathi

INGREDIENTS

600 ml thick coconut milk
125 g sugar
4 egg whites
pinch of salt
100 g fresh coconut, grated
2 tablespoons crushed peanuts
2 tablespoons sweet corn kernels

Set aside 4 tablespoons of the coconut milk. Place the remainder in a pan, add the sugar and stir over a moderate heat until the sugar has dissolved, then lower heat and simmer gently for 5 minutes.

In a bowl whisk the egg whites until they form soft peaks, then stir into the hot coconut milk. Continue to stir for 30 seconds, then remove pan from the heat. Allow to cool, then chill in the refrigerator for 30 minutes.

When cold, add the reserved coconut milk and the grated coconut. Transfer the mixture to an ice tray, or shallow freezer bowl, and leave for at least 2 hours, stirring every 40 minutes.

Remove from the freezer for 10 minutes before serving with a topping of crushed peanuts and sweet corn kernels.

Sticky Rice and Mango

Khao Niew Mamuang

INGREDIENTS

150 g glutinous rice
2 ripe mangoes
175 ml thick coconut milk
pinch of salt
3 tablespoons sugar

Soak the rice overnight, then drain and steam until tender.

Pour the coconut milk into a saucepan and bring to the boil. Add the salt and sugar and stir until the sugar has dissolved, then allow to cool before pouring over the rice. Fold until thoroughly mixed.

Halve the mangoes, scoop out the flesh and cut into small chunks. Arrange the rice onto individual serving platters and place a few chunks of mango at the side.

Water Chestnuts with Coconut Sauce

Tab Tim Krob

INGREDIENTS

300 g water chestnuts
1 teaspoon pink food colouring
450 g sugar
10 fresh jasmine
200 g potato flour
400 ml coconut milk
pinch of salt

Dice the water chestnuts and place in a bowl.

Mix the food colouring with 175 ml of water, pour over the water chestnut dice and leave for 20 minutes, then add the sugar and bring to the boil. Lower heat and stir until the sugar has dissolved, then remove from the heat and leave to cool. Add the jasmine petals and set aside for 10 minutes.

Drain the diced water chestnut and pat dry, then dredge in the flour. Reserve the syrupy liquid.

In a saucepan, bring water to the boil, add the water chestnut and cook until it floats to the surface, then remove with a slotted spoon and place immediately in a bowl of iced water.

Warm the coconut milk over a low heat until the milk reduces and thickens, then stir in the salt, remove from the heat and leave to cool.

To serve, divide the diced chestnut into individual bowls and pour on the syrup. Add the coconut milk and a little crushed ice.

Coconut Rolls with Sticky Rice

Khnom Neaw

INGREDIENTS

5 tablespoons cooked rice

1 tablespoon oil

450 g sticky rice flour

few drops of red, green and yellow food
  colourings

275 g fresh coconut, finely grated

425 g palm sugar

Spread the cooked rice on a tray and dry in a
low oven for 2 hours.

Heat the oil in a pan and fry the rice until
golden brown, then remove with a slotted spoon
and drain on kitchen paper.

Mix the flour with approximately 200 ml of tepid
water and knead until the dough is thick and
rubbery, then divide into three portions and place
each in a separate bowl.

Add a different colouring to each bowl and
mix well, then, using the hands, shape into small
sausage-shape rolls.

Bring a saucepan of water to the boil, add the
dumplings and cook until they rise to the surface,
then remove with a slotted spoon and drain on
kitchen paper.

Allow to cool, then coat evenly with the grated
coconut, arrange on a serving plate and surround
with the pieces of crispy rice.

Place the palm sugar in a small saucepan, then
add 3 tablespoons water and bring to the boil.
Lower heat and simmer until the sugar has dissolved,
then pour into a bowl and serve as a dipping sauce.

PHOTOGRAPH OVERLEAF

BAMBOO SHOOT
Cream-coloured, conical-shaped vegetable, best bought in cans available in many supermarkets. When bought fresh the outer skin has to be removed before boiling for a considerable time.

BEAN SPROUTS
The sprouts of the green mung bean which need a minimal of cooking time. Used a great deal in stir-frys and readily available.

BLACK MUSHROOMS
Generally known as Chinese mushrooms, they are sold dried and need to be soaked in warm water before using, after which the hard stems are usually discarded. The flavour is unique and there is really no acceptable substitute but they are readily available in Asian food stores and markets.

CHILLIES
Fresh and dried chillies play a major role in Thai cooking and the quantities used (regardless of what a recipe may suggest) depends on personal taste. For 'average' palates it is generally wise to discard the seeds before using. (See also page 6)

COCONUT MILK
Where fresh coconuts are available, the milk is obtained by grating the flesh of a mature (brown) coconut and squeezing with water. On average, the flesh of one coconut squeezed with 75 ml of water will produce the thick milk, most frequently referred to in the recipes. Should a thinner milk be called for, the process should be repeated one or more times. The liquid from the young (green) coconut is correctly known as coconut water and is seldom used in Thai cooking. If preferred, coconut cream and milk is available frozen, dried or in cans from most supermarkets.

CORIANDER
An essential ingredient in any Thai kitchen. The seeds, roots and leaves are all used and are readily available. Parsley is a member of the same 'family' but is not an acceptable substitute.

CURRY LEAVES
Small, aromatic leaves which are best bought fresh, but if these are not available use the dried variety.

FISH SAUCE
A salty brown sauce with a strong flavour. There are a number of varieties some more pungent and spicy than others. Should be used sparingly.

FIVE SPICE POWDER
A strong seasoning made from equal quantities of black peppercorns, fennel seeds, cinnamon bark, star anise and cloves.

GALANGAL
A member of the ginger family but with a distinctive spicy-peppery taste. Regular root ginger is not an acceptable substitute.

GARLIC
The cloves of the Thai garlic are smaller than the Western variety but there is no discernable taste difference. The skins have a light pinkish tint and are generally not removed before chopping or crushing.

GLUTINOUS RICE
A long-grained variety of rice which, despite its name, is gluten-free. However, it becomes very sticky when cooked and is most often used in desserts.

KAFFIR LIME
An Asian lime, somewhat larger than the more familiar variety. It has a dark green 'knobbly' skin and a sharp, aromatic flavour. The skin, leaves and juice are all used in Thai cooking and are generally available in Thai provision stores and many Asian markets.

LEMON GRASS
An aromatic grass with a small bulbous root, which, when crushed adds a strong lemon flavour. Has over the past few years become available in many Western supermarkets. Grated lemon peel makes a poor substitute.